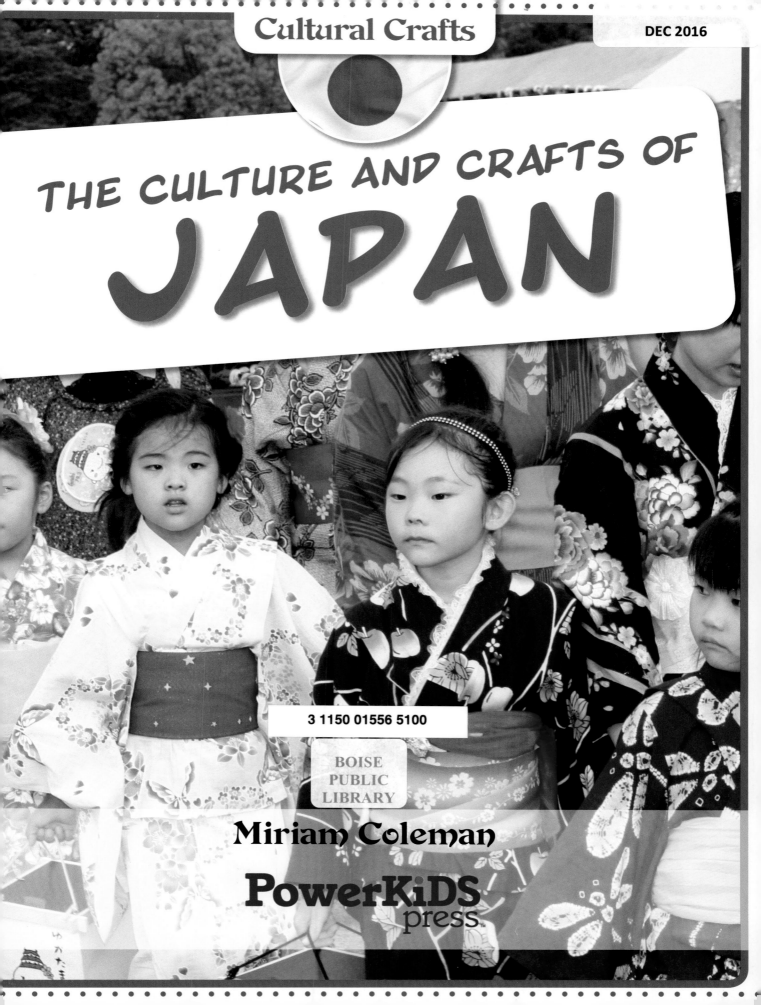

THE CULTURE AND CRAFTS OF JAPAN

Miriam Coleman

PowerKiDS
press

Published in 2016 by **The Rosen Publishing Group, Inc.**
29 East 21st Street, New York, NY 10010

Developed and produced for Rosen by BlueAppleWorks Inc.

Art Director: T. J. Choleva
Managing Editor for BlueAppleWorks: Melissa McClellan
Designer: Joshua Avramson
Photo Research: Jane Reid
Editor: Rachel Stuckey
Craft Artisans: Jane Yates (p. 7, 23), Jerrie McClellan (p. 13, 29)

Photo Credits:
Cover top left Samart Mektippachai/Shutterstock; cover top middle left Sofarina79/Shutterstock; cover top middle right
Perati Komson/Shutterstock; cover top right KPG Payless2/Shutterstock; cover middle Joshua Avramson/Shutterstock images;
cover bottom images, p. 6–7, 12–13, 22–23, 28–29 Austen Photography; cover top, title page top Marques/Shutterstock;
back cover, p. 4 top Arid Ocean/Shutterstock; title page, 15 right Corpse Reviver/Creative Commons; p. 4 left Walkdragon/
Dreamstime; p. 5 left Tanjala Gica/Shutterstock; p. 5 middle violetblue/Shutterstock; p. 5 left Tktktk/Dreamstime; p. 8–9
top Koichi Kamoshida/Keystone Press; p. 8 Ian Buswell/Keystone Press; p. 10 top Tranpan23/Creative Commons; p. 10
bottom KPG_Payless/Shutterstock; p. 11 left Francesco Libassi/Keystone Press; p. 11 right Kenichiro Seki/Keystone Press;
p. 11 top akiyoko/Shutterstock; p. 14 top Japanexperterna/Creative Commons; p. 14 bottom, 20 bottom Kok Leng Yeo/
Creative Commons; p. 15 left Yasu/Creative Commons; p. 16 top Lucian Milasan/Dreamstime; p. 16 bottom Nesnad/Creative
Commons; p. 17 top left Sixgimic/Creative Commons; p. 17 bottom left izamon/Shutterstock; p. 17 right Tibori /Dreamstime;
p. 18 top Mahroch/Dreamstime; p. 18 bottom Tooykrub/Shutterstock; p. 19 left, 19 right 663highland/Creative Commons;
p. 20 top Kobby Dagan/Dreamstime; p. 21 left, 24–25 top Cowardlion/Dreamstime; p. 21 right Wdeon/Dreamstime; p. 24
bottom kazoka/Shutterstock; p. 25 left Asiantraveler/Dreamstime; p. 25 right Veronika Synenko/Shutterstock; p. 26 top
Sean Pavone/Dreamstime; p. 26 bottomXXXXX; p. 27 left Maria Vazquez/Dreamstime; p. 27 right Attila Jandi/Dreamstime.

Cataloging-in-Publication-Data
Coleman, Miriam.
The culture and crafts of Japan / by Miriam Coleman.
p. cm. — (Cultural crafts)
Includes index.
ISBN 978-1-4994-1125-6 (pbk.)
ISBN 978-1-4994-1135-5 (6 pack)
ISBN 978-1-4994-1163-8 (library binding)
1. Japan — Juvenile literature. 2. Japan — Social life and customs — Juvenile literature.
3. Handicraft — Japan — Juvenile literature. I. Coleman, Miriam. II. Title.
DS806.C58 2016
952—d23

Manufactured in the United States of America
CPSIA Compliance Information: Batch #WS15PK For Further Information contact: Rosen Publishing, New York, New York at 1-800-237-9932

Contents

The Country of Japan

Japan

Japan is a nation in East Asia made up of thousands of islands. Japan lies between the North Pacific Ocean and the Sea of Japan, and its closest neighbors are Korea, Russia, China, and Taiwan. Japan is small in size; the country is smaller than the state of California in the United Staes, but it has the tenth highest population in the world. More than 13 million people live in Japan's capital, Tokyo.

The crane is a symbol of longevity and good luck in Japan. About 1,000 red-crowned cranes live in the country.

Modern Japan

Japan is believed to have been founded in 660 BCE, but people have lived on the islands since 30,000 BCE. Ancient traditions are still an important part of life in Japan, but the country is very modern and forward-looking. Japan is famous for its **innovations** in **technology**. Japan has the world's largest electronic goods industry and the third largest automobile industry. The transportation system in Japan is one of the most advanced in the world. High-speed bullet trains zoom across the country at speeds over 190 miles per hour (300 km/h).

Japan's government is a **constitutional monarchy** where citizens vote for members of **parliament**. The head of state is the prime minister and the Emperor of Japan holds a symbolic and ceremonial role.

Both ancient traditions and modern technology are part of Japanese culture today.

Craft to Make

Origami is the traditional Japanese art of paper folding. It began as a religious and ceremonial practice of monks in the 6th century. By the 17th century, when paper was more widely available, origami became a common pastime.

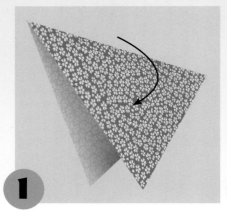

1

Head: Fold the paper in half to make a triangle. Make a good crease by pressing your finger along the fold line.

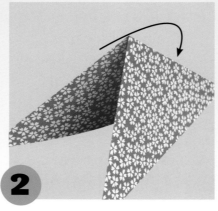

2

Fold the paper in half again. Make a good crease and then open the fold.

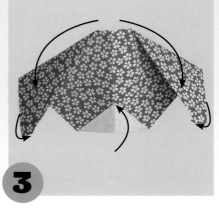

3

Fold both ends of the triangle down. Fold the tips of both ends back. Fold the tip of the triangle up on both sides.

You'll Need

2 square pieces of origami or other colored paper

Black marker

Tape

Googly eyes (optional)

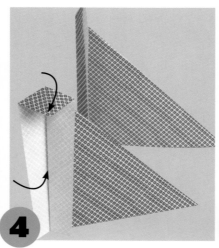

4

Body: Fold second piece of the paper in half, to form a triangle. Fold one side of the triangle over at the end. Open the fold and push the tip down.

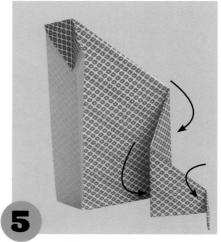

5

Fold the other end of the triangle three times to make the tail.

6

Draw or glue eyes to the face. Draw a nose. Tape the head to the body.

The Golden Week

Japanese people celebrate holidays throughout the year that are connected to events in the nation's history. Many of these holidays are during the same week in spring, known as Golden Week. Golden Week is the longest vacation period of the year for many Japanese people. Japanese families often go on trips during the break.

Golden Week begins with Showa Day on April 29th, the birthday of the late Emperor Hirohito, who ruled Japan from 1926 until 1989.

The Reigning Emperor Akihito and Empress Michiko try to bring the Imperial Family closer to the Japanese people.

The Japanese people use the Golden Week holiday to travel and visit interesting places.

Celebrating the Constitution

On May 3rd, Japan celebrates Constitutional Memorial Day to mark the day in 1947 when the country's new constitution took effect. All over the country there are festivals with parades, concerts, and kite flying. Greenery Day is celebrated on May 4th to show appreciation for the blessings of nature by planting trees.

The constitution is also celebrated on November 3rd for National Culture Day. The new constitution was officially announced on this day in 1946. The holiday celebrates the constitution's ideals of peace and freedom. Many festivals are held throughout the country for National Culture Day with art exhibitions, parades, and award ceremonies. At the Imperial Palace in Tokyo, the Emperor presents Order of Culture to people who have made outstanding contributions in culture, art, and science.

Children's Day

Japan's festive Golden Week ends with a special holiday for children on May 5th. On Children's Day families celebrate the growth, happiness, and personalities of their sons and daughters. Originally called *Tango no Sekku*, this was traditionally a holiday celebrating boys only. A separate holiday called *Hinamatsuri* or "Dolls' Day" celebrated girls on March 3. In 1948, the May 5th holiday was renamed *Kodomo no Hi* and became a day to celebrate all children.

Children's Day is a special day for parents to celebrate their children's unique personalities.

Floating Carps

Families observe Children's Day by hanging colorful streamers in the shape of carp from flagpoles and decorating their homes with iris, herbs, Samurai warrior dolls, and Samurai helmets. Children star in traditional plays and compete in a special Kids' Olympics held at Tokyo's National Kasumigaoka Stadium.

Families also celebrate Children's Day by eating special foods. One of these foods, *kashiwa mochi*, is a rice cake stuffed with sweet red bean paste and steamed in an oak leaf for good fortune. Another special dish is *chimaki*, which is made of sweet rice stuffed with meat or bean paste, mixed with walnuts, and steamed in bamboo leaves.

Children often dress in traditional costumes when celebrating Children's Day.

Craft to Make • • • • • • • • • • •

Families in Japan celebrate Children's Day by flying carp-shaped streamers called *koinobori*. Carp are a symbol of determination and strength because they swim upstream. Families fly one carp streamer for each child in the household.

1 Cut about 50 ovals from colored paper. Cut the ovals in half. The fish scale shape is an oval cut in half. These will be the fish scales.

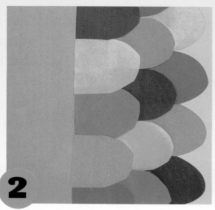

2 Cut a piece of posterboard 15 inches by 13 inches (38 cm by 33 cm). Apply glue along the short side and attach a row of scales. Continue making rows, overlapping the scales until you are 5 inches (13 cm) from the edge.

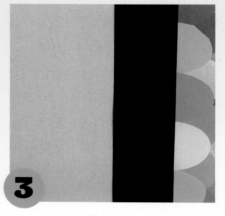

3 Cut a strip of black paper 1 ½ inches by 13 inches (4 cm by 33 cm). Place double-sided tape on one side and attach it over where the scales and body meet.

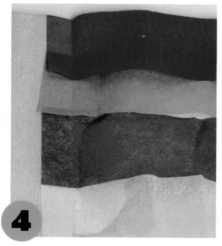

4 Cut 14 strips of tissue paper about 2 inches by 18 inches (5 cm by 46 cm). Glue or tape the strips to the edge of the board, underneath the scales.

5 Roll your poster board into a tube and tape it together. Put tape on the inside as well as the outside. Glue googly eyes above the black strip. Punch two holes at the top and tie a string through the holes. Put tape over the string and holes on the inside.

You'll Need

Poster board
Colored paper
Scissors
Tissue paper
Hole punch
String
Glue
Transparent tape
Double-sided tape
Googly eyes (2)

Religious Festivals

Shinto festivals and rituals include many ancient traditions.

Shinto and Buddhism are Japan's two major religions. Shinto is as old as the Japanese culture, but Buddhism was imported from mainland Asia in the 6th century. The two religions have existed in harmony ever since. The Shinto religion celebrates nature and spirits. Buddhism follows the teachings of Siddhartha Gautama, who is the Buddha, or the "enlightened one."

Many Japanese Buddhists practice Shinto rituals. Both religions have festivals that bring people together to celebrate. Buddhist temples celebrate Buddha's birthday on April 8th, and many Shinto shrines hold festivals to celebrate the changing seasons.

Ghosts of the Past

One of the biggest religious celebrations of the year is the Buddhist festival of *Obon*, or *Bon*. Traditionally, the three-day holiday takes place around the 15th day of the 7th month of the lunar year. Some parts of Japan celebrate on August 15, and other parts celebrate on July 15.

It is also known as the Ghost Festival. According to Buddhist legend, the spirits of ancestors return during Obon. Many families leave their homes in cities to hold reunions in the countryside. They clean family burial grounds and build a bonfire to guide the spirits to the family home on the first night of the festival. They also light lanterns around a family altar and leave **vegetarian** meals for their ancestors. At the end of the festival, when the ancestors' spirits have returned to paradise, communities celebrate with folk dances called *Bon Odori* set to the music of drums and flutes.

Matsuri

A *matsuri* is a local festival held at a Shinto shrine. There are many different *matsuri* because each shrine celebrates its own. The *matsuri* may celebrate the local shrine's deity, the season, or a historical event. *Matsuri* can happen at any time, but most local festivals happen around traditional holidays, like Obon. An important part of local festivals are processions. The local shrine's *kami* or deity is carried through the town. Every festival has its own characteristics. Some festivals are calm and quiet but others are noisy with lots of energy.

Bon Odori is a style of dancing performed during Obon to welcome the spirits of the ancestors.

During some *matsuri* there are processions with beautiful large floats.

15

New Year Celebrations

Streets are covered in decorations for the New Year's celebrations.

The celebration of the New Year is the most important holiday in Japan. It is a time to start fresh after the hard work and challenges of the year before. Japanese families clean their houses thoroughly to prepare for the New Year. Then they decorate with pine branches on their gates and flower arrangements inside. After working hard to complete all their chores, families enjoy a late-night New Year's Eve snack of soba noodles made from buckwheat.

A kadomatsu is a traditional pine branch decoration that is placed in front of homes to welcome ancestral spirits at the New Year.

Welcoming New Year

At midnight on New Year's Eve, Japan rings with the sound of bells. Every Buddhist temple in the country strikes its bronze bell 108 times to mark the New Year. Early the next morning, many people go to worship at Shinto shrines. At home, families celebrate with a ceremony that involves drinking a special sake, or rice wine, and eating a clear soup with a piece of rice cake called *o-zoni*. There is also a special New Year's feast called *osechi ryori* including foods such as pickled herring roe, grilled fish, black soybeans, radishes, and lotus roots, all stacked in pretty boxes.

The New Year is also a time to get in touch with friends and family by sending out beautiful printed cards called *nengajō*.

Osechi ryori feast is tasty and colorful.

On January 2 the Emperor gives a New Year's speech. Crowds gather to hear the speech and cheer for the Imperial family.

Nengajō Cards Craft

Japanese nengajō or New Year's greetings cards are a fun, easy, and great way to send well wishes to your friends and family.

Step One: Buy or create your own nengajō.

You can pick up preprinted nengajō in stationary stores. There are many different designs to choose from but most will have a version of the zodiac sign for the upcoming year.

2016 is the year of the Monkey, and 2017 will be the year of the Rooster. Use the proper symbol if creating your own! Some people like to include photos of themselves or their family as well.

Step Two: Write your message.

Once you've made your nengajō, include a personal message. Nengajō cards in Japan are used to say thank you to families, friends and neighbors for their support during the previous year.

HAPPY NEW YEAR!

Architecture of Japan

The inside of a Japanese home is very different from North American homes.

Traditional Japanese architecture is in harmony with nature and values a sense of calm. Japanese homes were built for a climate with hot summers and plenty of rain. The houses are also open to nature. Long, gently curved overhanging roofs made of baked clay tiles help keep the interior dry during heavy rains, and the floor is raised off the damp ground. One of the most interesting features of traditional Japanese houses are the walls made from sliding panels with wood frames covered in thick paper. These walls can be moved to make rooms larger or smaller. The sliding walls also keep fresh air moving through the house and allow in plenty of sunlight.

Tokyo is a city of modern architecture.

Ancient Designs

Religious shrines and temples are an important part of Japan's architectural traditions. The oldest Shinto shrines are often simple rectangular buildings with thatched roofs. Buddhist architecture, which first came to Japan around the sixth century, reflects the influence of its Chinese and Korean roots. Pagodas, or towers with many levels of roofs, are an important structure in Buddhist architecture.

Japan's tradition of architecture continues in modern buildings and skyscrapers, such as the imaginative Mode Gakuen Cocoon Tower in Tokyo.

Japanese Gardens

Gardens are an important part of Japanese architecture. This reflects how special nature is in Japanese culture. Japanese gardens are meant to remind us of natural landscapes and include slopes, sand, rock formations, and waterfalls. Zen gardens are a special type of garden with only rocks and sand. The simple elements in a Zen garden symbolize the land and ocean and are meant to encourage contemplation.

The pagoda of Hōryū-ji, or the Temple of the Flourishing Law, is the oldest wooden building in the world.

Japanese Zen gardens are famous for their harmony and simplicity.

Traditional Clothing

Festivals are a good time to see the different types of traditional dress in Japan.

Japan has a long history of **textile** arts. Japanese design has influenced fashion all across the world. The country's beautifully woven and printed fabrics can be seen in its most famous traditional garment, the kimono.

Japanese Kimonos

Kimonos are long, loose robes with wide sleeves. They have no buttons or other fasteners and are tied at the waist with a wide sash called an obi. Kimonos are worn by both men and women, but there are differences in the styles. Most men's kimonos are black or dark colored. On formal occasions, men will wear a half-length jacket called a *haori* and wide silk trousers called *hakama* along with the kimono. Women's kimonos can be brightly colored, with a variety of different sleeve lengths, fabrics, and designs meant for special occasions.

Kimonos are not very practical for everyday wear, so most Japanese people only wear them on holidays or during traditional arts performances. On less formal occasions, many people wear a more comfortable, lighter cotton version called a *yukata*.

People often wear traditional kimonos for their weddings.

Coming of Age Day

The second Monday of January each year is Coming of Age Day in Japan. This holiday celebrates young men and women who have turned 20 in the past year and are now legally adults with the right to vote. Municipal governments all over the country hold Coming of Age Day ceremonies to mark the new rights and responsibilities of the young people. Men usually dress in modern suits for the occasion, but many women wear special formal kimonos called *furisode*.

Coming of Age Day ceremonies have always been part of Japanese culture.

Craft to Make • • • • • • • • • •

Handheld fans are part of traditional Japanese clothing. The beautifully decorated fans can be used to create a cool breeze when it's hot, but they are also important in religious ceremonies and traditional arts such as Kabuki theater.

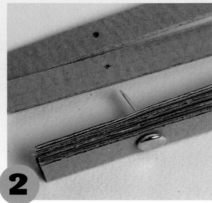

1 Measure and cut 7 strips of cardboard. The strips should be 1/2 inch wide by 9 ½ inches long (1.3 cm by 24 cm). Make a mark on each strip 1 ½ inches (4 cm) from the end.

2 Use a pushpin to make a hole at each mark. Twist the pushpin in each strip to widen the hole. Put the fastener through each hole in the strip.

3 Close the fastener when all the strips are on. Spread the strips out.

4 Draw a semicircle around the top edge of the strips. About 3 inches (7.6 cm) from the fastener, draw a semicircle in the space between the strips. Remove the strips and cut out the paper along the semicircles.

5 Spread the strips evenly and glue or tape the strips to the back of the paper. Carefully fold the paper at the edge of each strip. Attach a tassle to the fastener.

You'll Need

Cardboard (thin)

Pencil and ruler

Scissors

Pushpin

Patterned paper, 11" x 17" (28 cm x 43 cm)

Glue or double-sided tape

Fastener (1)

Glue

Yarn tassle (optional)

22

Japanese Fan

Famous Japanese Cuisine

Rice has been **cultivated** in Japan since at least 300 BCE and holds an important place in the culture. Many traditional festivals and holidays celebrated planting and harvesting rice. Rice is such a central part of traditional cuisine that two Japanese words for "meal" are *gohan* and *meshi*, which both mean "cooked rice."

Typical Japanese meals also include a variety of side dishes called *okazu*. Okazu may include grilled fish, boiled vegetables, and meat, as well as battered and fried fish or vegetables called *tempura*, and soup made from a soybean paste called *miso*.

The Japanese use wooden chopsticks to eat their meals.

Sushi

Seafood of all kinds is popular in Japan, but one of the country's most famous ways to eat it is sushi. Sushi has a base of rice seasoned with vinegar, either formed into a small mound or rolled up with seaweed. Sushi is often topped with slices of raw fish, but it can also be made with vegetables or cooked seafood. Sashimi is thin slices of raw fish without rice.

Famous Noodles

Noodle dishes are also very popular in Japan. Noodles can be ordered in restaurants, street stalls, and food stands on train platforms. The most famous varieties are soba, which are made from buckwheat, thick wheat noodles called udon, and thin wheat noodles called ramen.

The city of Osaka is famous for its street food. Many people wait in line at the best street stalls.

Favorite Sports in Japan

Baseball is so popular in Japan that fans are often surprised to hear that baseball is America's "national pastime."

One of Japan's most beloved sports is baseball. There are 12 professional teams in Japan and they all draw cheering crowds to stadiums throughout the country. Students of all ages play on school teams. Soccer has also developed a major following in Japan since a professional soccer league formed there in the 1990s.

Japan has dominated the Women's Baseball World Cup, winning every gold medal since 2008.

Martial Arts

Japan is home to a wide variety of traditional **martial arts** with a history going back many centuries. Sumo wrestling, which is often considered Japan's national sport, started more than 1,000 years ago. Sumo wrestlers try to push each other out of the ring or bring each other to the ground.

Judo, which means "the gentle way," is another popular form of Japanese martial arts. Invented in Japan in the 19th century, Judo takes advantage of an opponent's strength by turning it against him or her. Judo became an official Olympic sport in 1964. Other popular martial arts in Japan include *kendo*, a form of fencing using bamboo swords, and *kyudo*, a form of archery.

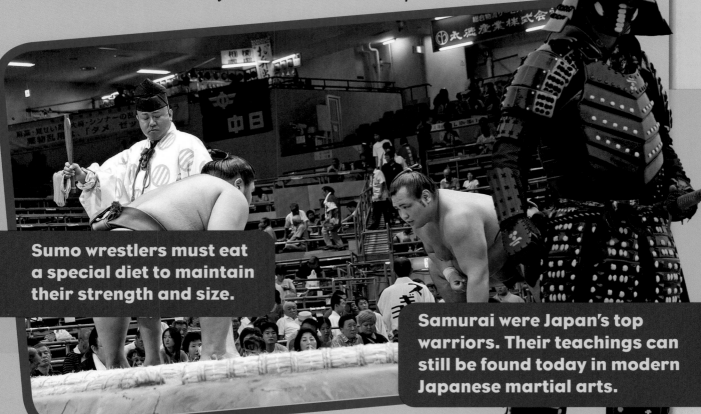

Sumo wrestlers must eat a special diet to maintain their strength and size.

Samurai were Japan's top warriors. Their teachings can still be found today in modern Japanese martial arts.

27

The samurai were a special class of professional soldiers who ruled Japan from the 12th to the 19th centuries. Samurai used many types of weapons including bows and arrows, spears, and the famous samurai sword. Samurai followed a strict warrior's code called *bushido*.

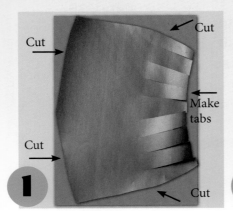

1

Trim the poster board so that it is about 13.5 inches (34.5 cm) wide and the length wraps around your head. Trim the edges from the corners, as seen in the image. Then cut nine 5-inch (13 cm) tabs from the top edge.

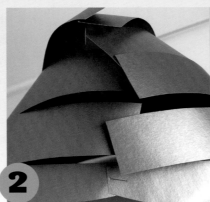

2

Staple the two outside tabs together as shown. Continue with the next two tabs, making sure they overlap the tabs below. The last tab is stapled on top, overlapping all the tabs.

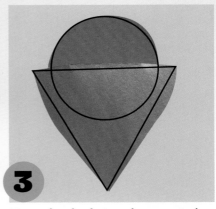

3

To make the brim, draw a circle 4 inches (10 cm) across on a piece of poster board. Then draw a triangle by making a line across the middle of the circle. Make a mark 5 inches (13 cm) above the line, outside the circle. Draw two lines from this mark to just outside the half circle, to complete the triangle. Cut out the triangle-semicircle shape, or use the pattern on page 30.

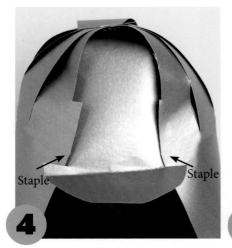

4

Cut two small slits on either side of the circle and fold the circle up. Slide the brim into place and staple it to the helmet. Tape the tip of the triangle to the inside of the helmet.

5

Use patterns on pages 30-31 to draw and cut out a sword and a U shape as above. Tape the sword to the U shape. Glue or tape the sword and U shape to the helmet above the brim. Decorate the helmet with decorative tape and self-stick gems.

You'll Need

Poster board (2 sheets) gold and silver 18" x 24" (46 cm X 61 cm)

Scissors

Pencil or marker

Ruler

Stapler

Tape

Decorative tape

Self-stick gems

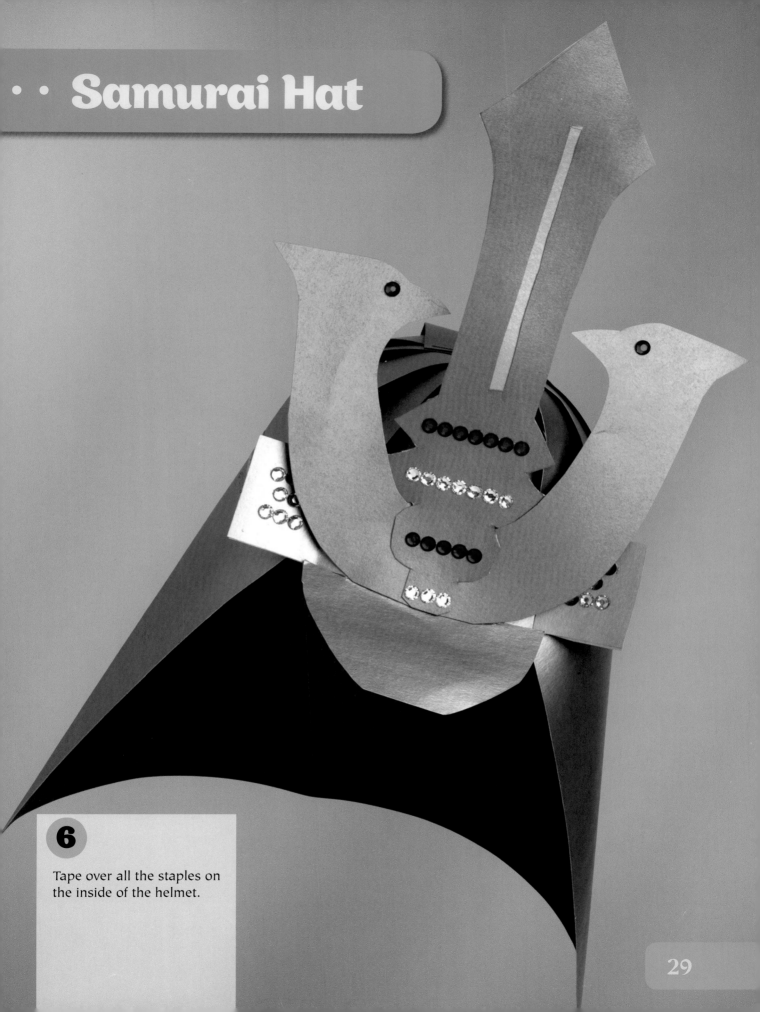

•• Samurai Hat

6

Tape over all the staples on the inside of the helmet.

GLOSSARY

constitution A document that explains the basic rules for a country's laws and government.

constitutional monarchy A system of government that includes both a king or queen and elected leaders.

cultivate To grow a plant in large quantities.

innovation The creation of something new.

martial art A sport or skill that came from the practice of self-defense or military skills.

parliament The group of elected leaders who vote on laws.

technology Machines or tools created from scientific knowledge, now usually involving electronics and computers.

textile Woven cloth.

vegetarian Food that does not include meat.

Sword and brim patterns for the Samurai helmet craft.

FOR MORE INFORMATION

Further Reading

Catel, Patrick. *Countries Around the World: Japan.*
Portsmouth, NH: Heinemann Publishing, 2012.

Florence, Debbi Michiko. *Japan: Over 40 Activities to
Experience Japan — Past and Present.*
Nashville, TN: Williamson Books, 2009.

Otowa, Rebecca. *My Awesome Japan Adventure:
A Diary about the Best 4 Months Ever!*
North Clarendon, VT: Tuttle Publishing, 2014.

Phillips, Charles. *National Geographic
of the World: Japan.* Des Moines, IA: National Geographic
Children's Books, 2009.

**U-shape pattern
for the Samurai
helmet craft.**

Websites

Due to the changing nature of Internet links, PowerKids Press
has developed an online list of websites related to the subject
of this book. This site is updated regularly. Please use this link
to access the list: **www.powerkidslinks.com/cc/japan**

INDEX